Acknowledgement

I would firstly like to acknowledge and thank my husband, Corey.
Without you, this book would not be the reality it is today.
You are my number one supporter, my rock and my life.
Thankyou for saving me each and every day.

I would secondly like to thank my two baby boys, Mason and Jamie.
You have brought light into the lives of all who meet you.

To my illustrator - you brought my vision to life, thank you.
To the New South Wales Police force in its entirety - thank you
for the support and protection you provide each and everyone.

To Blacktown Police Station, the place where my policing
journey began, especially the intelligence team.

Lastly, to my family and friends
(inside and outside of the police force)
thank you for supporting me through this journey,
especially Jenni and Martin.

For Corey.
You are our kid's hero.

Dedicated to
the brave New South Wales
Police Officers.
Thank you for your service.

About the author

A fun fact about me is that
I was a Police officer for close to 3 and
a half years. During my time
spent at the police academy in Goulburn,
I met my now husband, Corey.
Together we share two beautiful son's,
Mason and Jamie.

I have since resigned from
the New South Wales police force
and you can find me pursuing
a variety of hobbies, one of which
is writing children's books.

When he comes home,
I am so happy to see him
and run up to him
to give him a great BIG hug.

When he is working he has to carry so many tools, so that he will always be prepared.

Sometimes when he is working out, I like to join him. He helps to lift me up, so I can do a pull-up.

He helps to keep everyone safe.
Is there a time you remember
when your parents kept you safe?

When he is at work, he drives the police car to get to and from places.

The police car makes a very loud noise that is called a siren.

The siren is designed to help warn other drivers to give-way to the police car.

The police car also has flashing lights, kind of like the ones you would also see on an ambulance and fire brigade.

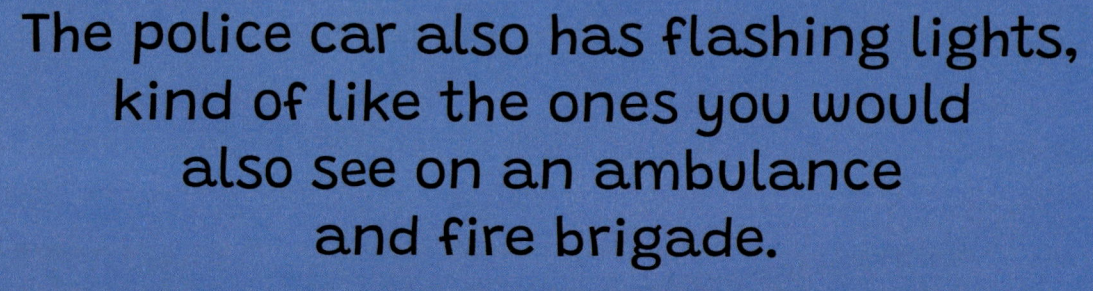

Can you spot the emergency vehicles?

Police Car

Ambulance

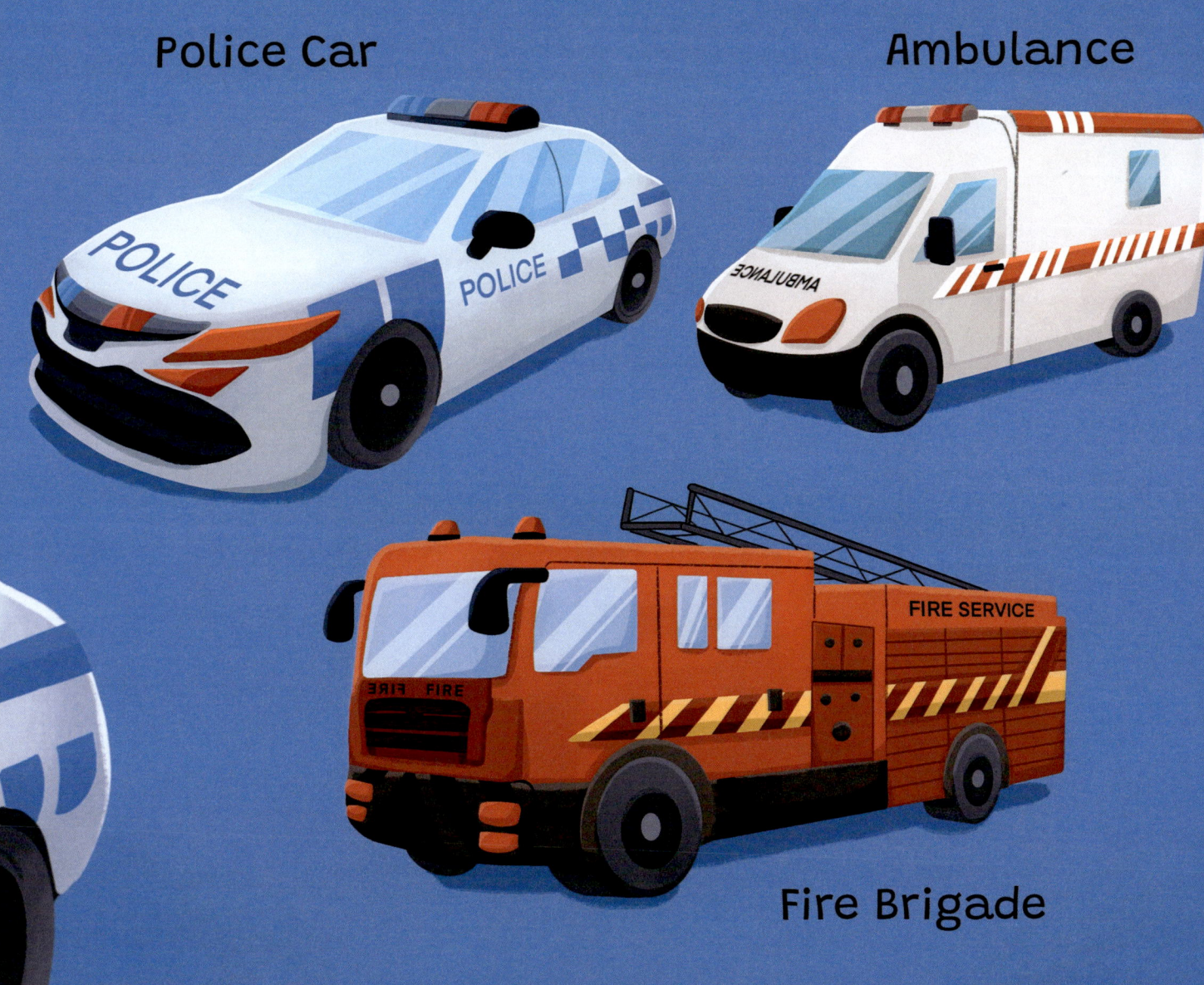

Fire Brigade

Sometimes it can be scary meeting a police officer for the first time. But they are all very friendly, so there is no need to be scared.

What should you do in case of an emergency?

Tell a parent/adult.

Call 000

Remain calm.

It is important to know what to do in case of an emergency. Follow the steps above during an emergency.

The purpose of this book is to educate young children about the very important role of being a police officer and what it involves.

www.ingramcontent.com/pod-product-compliance
Lightning Source LLC
Chambersburg PA
CBRC092340290426
44109CB00008B/173